January 2008

Don
all best
Ben

January 2008

Ben Mazer

DARK SKY BOOKS

Copyright © 2010 Ben Mazer

Published by Dark Sky Books
Seattle, Washington
All rights reserved.

www.darkskybooks.com

No part of this book may be reproduced in any form or by any electronic or mechanical means including information storage and retrieval systems, without permission in writing from the author and/or publisher.

Printed in the United States of America.

ISBN-13: 978-0-615-34305-1
ISBN-10: 0615343058

First Dark Sky Books Printing, 2010

Book design: Jesse Lutz

These poems, written in a short period of time after the death of Landis Everson, were never published because they were never sent to any magazines. I forgot that I wrote them, but the poems were saved because I sent them to Stephen Sturgeon.

January 2008

Prologue

Sometimes when circling around by lefts and rights
I count the friggin snowmen in my path.
Then multiplied by the divisive whites
of snowy flesh I do my poetry math.
Single flash exposures are the art
of memory in the museum of
decisions in December of the heart
where the new year ascribes to love.
Show me a snowman as bereft and bare
as my believing that in being there
I am my own man, though I may be yours
whether because existing out of doors
or because of also having no one
who I can turn to say or see a snowman.

Embarrassing the Gods

My urination violation
helped to pay for my vacation.
Oh do not ask what is it
when you make your mental visit,
quoth the raven, while my mental
escapades are accidental
only when I do not think it.
So I'm making you this trinket
in case you want to contemplate
our coinciding at this date.
I could not express it better
than by talking through your sweater
like an Indian chieftain or
a gentle army of wild boar.
All that I can do is wing it,
hoping back to me you'll sing it,
sometimes embarrassing the gods,
exposing all the inner thoughts
that make me want to
categorize them all in lots,
I think I can do.
When it is pouring in the noon
maybe it won't be too soon
to softly name
and itemize the groves of June.
Like a fire then will fame
enjoy its promise without shame.
Occidents of welter rudge

may discontinue to misjudge
the preening prom queen
and turn her quizzi-
cal extremptions to a quasi-
mathematically obscene
half exposition
on the strength of my position
and orgasms of myopic
caring for my biopic.

Homage

Betwixt you and me
is a tying of sea and sea
to where I outward can't recall
the being there I would foresee
when I met you; I was three
and couldn't yet need to forestall
your vying, lying further on
where the rocky mists repeat
the savage mariner's devout
interlocutions, and the sea
is implicating you with me.

I didn't tell you how much I
thought about or imagined your pussy
because of all the times you said
we'd never ever go to bed.

I like to imagine you my bride
which all the time I have to hide.

Dear Miss Poe, please grow your hair long
and spend your furlough prinking by the furlong,
cast honey pelts of doubt into the dong
of slinking evening. Let true love be wrong
and hang from cornices of misspent song.
Invent in traffic of your veins my trick
of listening before the voice's prick.
Oppose the throng of nothing in the tick
of painted evening. Languish in the kick
of sundry calendars besprinkling time.

Snaggly waggly went to fair,
saw the natty raccoon there.
When the raccoon went to play,
Snaggly waggly ran away.

Snaggly laid out estate to
several owners of the zoo.
Snaggly cut quick dividends
with her new established friends.

Underneath the laundry lines
the talking animal refines
Snaggly in her diary
Reported rabbit's courtesy.

Snaggly among the crocodiles,
Snaggly traveling miles and miles,
then settling to make her home
in the wilders of Wyom.

Dante

Dante looked at Beatrice
on the number 7 bus.
Out of the periphery
of her vision she could see
Dante. Then he got his friend
to sit between them and pretend
that Dante really looked at her,
that way keeping his love pure.
Then one day his lady died,
and she passed through him while he cried,
numbering his griefs for her
while yet she looked on demure.
She was like a ghostly king
on top of Dante who would sing
of what in Beatrice he saw,
of sweetnesses inspiring awe.
Now Dante is a ghost to us
who since must ride the 7 bus
hearing Dante echoing
lays of his lady king.

Mushroom Mountain

When you start watching again
you are in another movie
but the programming's the same.
Charlton Heston and William Shatner
are wearing white Roman robes
and beating this girl senseless.
Looking over the things to pack
and sniffing the goldleaf geraniums
washing your hands from the newspaper.
It is time to be in where the leopard waits
or coyotes for a dog in packs
smelling like you have just been there.
I don't want to answer loudly until dawn
but The Love-Ins have captivated
my circling around looking for someone like you.
It is I who am leaving Vivien Leigh
and when I return someone else's face
will be on the screen.
Charles Boyer will be handing Irene Dunne a rose.
I packed what little I had
gathering sometimes what the natives gave me
to be with you in this strange place in the mountains.

Above two automatic gates the rented ranch
looks like the set of Night of the Iguana,
sliding out under the stars where clay spittoons
mantle each tawdry lookout flooded with light
from fixtures on the wooden awnings
and by the pool, where secrecy within
filters and flows into ethereal starlight
where the prison blocks roaming signals
and the wireless connection sometimes fades
leaving the shards of pictures on a screen
that never stops playing movies like each other.
The top of the mountain prays that minimal phones
will elude the scent of boars and mountain lions
when the power plant goes out and rocks are falling.
The intiming appointments of town destroy the morning
because connections are not made at random
and the accountant assistant on her day off
is less static than the architect's lone laptop
hudding the breeze of the town marijuana smoker.
Everyone is friendly because it is windier
than motion for an integer by the ocean
where the stable fish get caught in dogs
and buying a cup of coffee somewhat cheaper.
It's free to talk about a quarter million
and the har har makes me make you happy
because you can't sell what I buy with my love
attacking the natives relentlessly for not examining
everything that's printed on the subject
because the works of my friends are immortal.

I don't scatter but lick and suck your ashes
remembering how much you loved me yell at you
that I would die before you would decide
one single part of it, how I taught my pride
to fall over an edge recycling love.
You are my Frankenstein.
But I am scared to read what you unwrote
of words we told you, also knowing you
had caught me in my own creation.

I hunt the houses where you left your mark
in wooden objects and paint surfaces
for him or her. The hesitating dark
unveils your love in words that never cease
illuminating rooms that we have left
or you left earlier, replaying scenes
where secrets whisper louder and arrest
the underground oblivion of our dreams.
Because you put a gun to love my love
dies full of bullets under the plane tree.
You are laughing almost from above
at nothing really, what we choose to see
because you meant in doing what you did
the full extent of love before you died.

All the butter in your sweater
sweats the necktie resolutions
of my envy. I'll feel better
when these inept tacit collusions
forgiving speech rest on the water
where the row of tinkling lights incites
interior euphorias to the patter
of brilliant panthers and night moderates
conclusive currents, time analysis
where fur blurred gropes, berates to hesitate
a darning dimple of my foreblent hopes.

A City of Angels

When he came back his family had moved
into the city. Nothing was the same.
In deepest winter he left poverty
to try his fortune in a newer time.
At first he preached himself more ardent learning
and stalked the chrysalis of stationary
star and moonlight. Shards of static groves
of ice in legendary lattices
of light and shadow thinking of him grew
into tall spires and towers to undo
the love he had projected. The ballet
of loss and yearning pricked the vacant rug
around the edges of his promises
with lunar urgency that flounced the lid
of calendars and planning and the stark
recesses of a gallop in the sky.
He had not yet begun, and couldn't die.
A thought was born, and in that thought a city.
The simple palace of the pregnant rain
drew him much nearer and though unexposed
those few lost evenings into a deeper night
forever left untold in vacuous ports
of patterned peering. Sleep's society
of utterance revolved on its own course.
The rented seatings of the sky that blew
into new friendship clattered on the ceiling.

If you weren't going to let me tell you I love you,
what were you doing writing a poem for me in the first place?
Do I get tired of waiting for someone to understand me?
Take any of your gym shorts down to the penitentiary
and reduce for me your Frenchman into a fire hose
for my pepperoni pizza. I'm hairless if I care.
My thoughts are a fuzzy wuzzy fireplace atmosphere
of doing you and not doing what I'm told.

Buds. Ice. Pines. Windows. Babes. New year.
Elephant. Window seat. Octagonal. Reflection.
Silence. Shuddering. Hammering. Welcoming.
Division. Fragmentation. Peace. Visitor.
Township. Echoing. Report. Christening.
Baptism. Recollection of foretelling.
Schism. Prism. Arrival. Windless current.
Opportunity. Decision. Incantation. Invitation.
Darkness. Listening. Loosening. Lightening.
There is nothing like it. It is not what is it.
You know how I want you to know.
Listen to me unhooking your brastrap.

Cookies and Lamictal

The undershirt of my imagination stinks
with always persuading sheerly by tone
the remembered dipsticks of our latter winter
when to atone for me you went alone
to veering vetters of the current cutter.
I want to see, want to see Tyrone
Power play Philip Marlowe.
Cut straight to the bone
I am not write. Won't be this winter.

Have nothing left to tell except what is it
Cassandra Nelson wouldn't be this season's
ice show girl in my imagination
and I am left without a rhyme or reason.

Frankenstein the aviator flew
eleven feet indoors. No one ever knew.
He had perfected the bearings of steel
and got his airplane off the ground by feel.
He liked his poetry, and he liked Vienna,
and he liked a simple girl called Hannah.
She would mend his socks and cook his stew
while silently his mathematics grew.
All this took place before 1911
and was not published till 1927.
Those who knew him, who were very few
wondered at his strength of solitude.
He himself had written an etude
to celebrate the secrets of the nude.
Some of his students thought he might be gay.
But every winter he went away
to Austria and never said a word.
Life to him was something he had heard.

Because he adapted quickly to the cold
and partly knew the language of his dad,
the explorer on his vacation grew
to admire the limits of the land locked land.
Such stony rubbish beckoned at his hand
as sunset that was red and that was blue
to turn the key at evening and was sad.
The next day he'd be out there, being bold.

The Romantics

They printed more newspapers, filling them with words
they wanted to hear dictated in the office,
bought more paper to stack in folded files
ready to be sewn and distributed. In the windows
lists of their contributors topped the bright red SOLD OUT
that was duplicated in their prospectus. All the aisles
of the city's theatres were decked with nasty reporters
ready to see or say anything they saw.
But what was lovely was the things that filled the articles,
stories of ceilings flickered on in the dark,
mornings of travelers in small hotels,
the words of the university chancellor over tea,
simple chiaroscuros of the leisure hours,
consummate rejection of the belling towers.
People stopped into the offices and they sold
more than half of what they printed. Then
across the street at the saloon they gave
the rest away. Inside the saloon they read
the printed sheets out loud and planned to lure
better writers to write for the next issue.
They had read much Shakespeare, you can be sure.

Now they rest in several libraries.
They are not read, or even glanced over.
The horsechestnut whispers that you hurt me.
Something you loved to love me begins to love me.
The chief librarian goes unanswered.
No one cares that life isn't a book.
All the manuscript and special collections
grow hateful to the illegibly jealous.

for ss

Hashish in Mrs. Gardener's private boudoir
a private concert on Paderewski's piano
champagne flowing downstairs at the Christmas party
the cameras rolling and a guard was fired

Two nights later on the shift he missed
his friends were tied up in the radio room
by elderly, elite white Boston gangsters
who had a predilection for Vermeer

How many times I described Rembrandt's self portrait
at twenty to Japanese visitors
and now two Rembrandts have gone awfully absent
to the sounds of old world jazz in Boston's autumn

Take me there to stare at the blank spaces
of empty albums on the salon doors
and I will swear there were once art and culture
in the little rooms of Mrs. Gardener's salon

He saw the birdwatcher in the distance
raised the gun to his head, the woman yelled
"oh lord" the animals scattered and he fired.
A sameness of birds flew off in his direction.
A smart sheep learned to see a human dying.

Then he was headlines, a bullet's report.
Quotes of friends who'd seen his rise to fame.
A few appearances and a private library,
only the chief librarian never answered.

His poems stirred the old feeling underground
where love still made its signal word for love
and silent with their truth they passed around
declaratives like cheaper currency,

the coiling of the wind in groves of autumn,
an old vagrant fogging wiping and looking in.

The strokes were what first killed him instantly
He couldn't understand the poems he'd written
then his second collection was rejected
he destroyed his poems, and blew his brains out.
Always this hatred for the self would rise
to blacken an eye. He gave away his money
and fed the birds in a ratty sweater.
The panoply of operas befall
and instigate seclusion in his work.
The cities of the angels shall remember
electricity of word he'd underground.

This lovely lady likes to sit at home
and straighten knick knacks, paint a nook of wall.
I see her through the window hanging wires
and colored lights, perfect for the fall.
She has a regal bearing when she faces
another in our cluttered and cramped quarters.
She helped to shovel dog shit from the floor
of Melissa, one of the upstairs boarders.
Sometimes I give her space to play her flute,
drinking espressos at the local cafe.
Walking home it's cold and I want warmth
waiting for me silently within.

I always liked your candlelit family albums
after one had gone to sleep.
Trying hard not to laugh too loud
at pictures of everyone younger.
I always liked the music you put on
Sidney Bechet or Bessie Smith
as you drew me into the room without lights
where I described the stars that I saw
and you left loving for another evening.

The stars are glittering into the heaven
when you arrive. The sofa coverlets
lowered into place by bluebirds. A Ming vase
entertaining echoes reminds you of
where you have been. A magnolia grove
shuttered into shadow by the evening.
Gossamer epaulets of telling time
hang from your motion. Snapping fans
elucidate the view of match boxes.
Unguent breath requires a text of song.
A plectrum scattered at the old piano.

The long clock scores the epistles of reason
in the slow offices of the after midnight
rain plate and box camera of lace.
Someone's older expert whistle riddles
the dying of the printed artifact.
Love letters billow like an extra pillow.
Years of perfume count backwards secrecies.
Angels cluttered on the copper ceiling
paint mysteries of hope in promises
like ocean laughter. Circus is the year.
All the washed out calendars derive
from energy, spilling back into truth
like youth or lethargy until conspire
love lifted in explicatory lease.

She is the queen of dream and every time
she seems to screen the scene she takes a dim
view to what is being. Nerves are fraying
but this year no one else is saying
that it ought to be replaced with what has been.
With every guess her gambit grows more thin.
I align the eye with ordinary revery in a steady
exhalation of the ether that my buddy
wrote six sonnets for a maiden on.
There is no place to hide. C'est maintenant.
I place his order for a bride. I've lost my pride
and do not think that I shall take a bride
but will not know until I get inside.
I merely point out that she tanned my hide.

Picasso and Braque stripped off the top of talk
and sent each sidewise to the other down color
and under line into seeing. Cubes of words
replaced the pigments on their pallets
when they painted, went to town.
Town came to them. The towns of ports and cities.
And splintered in the brilliance of morning.
Braque went down to Picasso and his brush asked
what color is it that I must already visit?
Picasso painted the town, tone and town.
Both painted portraits of Kahnweiler.

The stitch and thimble like the laundry lines
require vacancy. No one affords
the genius in his wastebasket
when gin soaks the evenings.
The roof is bare and Katy there
but little to add. I huff and breathe
the stars that Matt is shaking with his eyes.

The honeymoons return to different tunes
under a cabinet peg previously unnoticed
but like all of the things that went before
in a simple wedding dress of white lace.
There is nothing in the cabinet, no biscuits
or champagne but just this elixir of love
under starlight the nectar of the gods
which the bride and groom assume to drink.
I am reminded of someone whom I talk to at night
when it is snowing out. There will be no school.
I only went to school once but have never returned.
I change the photos in the photo book
until it looks like you and me at Niagara
before Joseph Cotten visited there with Marilyn Monroe.

This madman is dreaming of a madman dreaming of a madman
The first madman meets the third madman in the second madman's dream
but turn out to be discussing the first madman until the fifth gets there.

When we first went out onto the water
I saw that you were talking to another
who came this way in the far time ago
but has receded. Loneliness moves slow
upon the bridges and the piers where love
remained unanswered while he was alive.
Now you are gone, and all your love for me
disappears then reappears where he
also is constant, suddenly I see
myself ardently ripple awkwardly.

Time goes on without a plan.
The trumps and trimmings
of the beautiful elite
go unrecorded. Laws of the estate
travel backwards, leave
me on my own, as with
a photograph of your sin.
March chaotically through August blown
doesn't reach me on the telephone
where I am engaged in rhyming
what I see with what I'm hearing.
So it has been recently said
all comes to nothing.
I am a number. Come here.
Do not let the rain
let us do anything but remember.

Hello! Today my bathtub
wants to go to the movies.
and a close friend of mine
wants to go with them.
But I say I am the movies
and as if to prove it
become Buster Keaton
or Mary Pickford.
It is raining
and very sexy
to have a movie
to think out loud about.
Let's all come here
talking in and out of it
to watch this thing together.

Books. I've had enough
and can't remember dates
or names or face. But I
remember what a thing is!
Come face to face with love
and the audible conflorescence
of manning a calendar, the spring
is juniper evocative, aglow
with needles of unbeing, hordes before
the endlessness of repetition
of timeless myth larger than its legend!

Her cautiousness he painted blue
so she could see it from the window
covered over with a blue haze
that stumped the streetlight.
Then she was his visitor
and never came again to say
the porticoes across the street
were dappled in the winter moon.
These indexes of where they stood
a crux for nothing, reminded
the armchair where to begin
consternating from the floor.

A leaf below the crust again
replete bodacious gathering
investing whom to bloom within
expostulating medicine
to how whoever whom so be
retarded in the water crest
impervious beyond the sea.

Calyx bounty hideous grave
interplanetary wave

Ralph Otter sat upon a rock
and taught a welkin how to talk.
When it came to two or three
welkins they were ordinary.
Ralph Otter taught them how to talk.
Ordinary welkins walk
under the table, ostrich-style.
The younger welkins aren't able.
Walking, talking, all in a pile.
The welkins Ralph Otter taught to talk.

Evaporate March revives cisterns

Frankenstein was often left alone,
and drew his plans upon a devil's throne.
A wreck of marriage made he in the time
his scientific studies drew unto the time.
When he was electric, he was free
to nurture life itself, most stormily.

Dracula was doubtful by dissent
and hardly cared to know what way he went
pursuing ladies safely in the dark
in the operatic public park.
Familiarly meticulous the count
illuminated weaved as if to mount
sideways the answer to the stuff of dreams
in grove-like shadows trinkling by the reams
across the garden window to the north
silence of hours well into the fourth.
He offers good wine but can't recall
who drank it with him in the fall.
At the opera he's debonair,
fixated on ladies' hair.
By the moon he drives them bats,
makes them all feel like cats,
giving in to his desire
because he fills the room with fire.
Yet the bookish side of him
sees to it that the lawn's trim,
which he never did before
in Budapest or Singapore.
London makes him really free.
Visits the Queen every Sunday.
Dracula, Dracula, are you free,
would you care to dance with me?
Maybe share a trance with me?
Instruct me. Be exemplary.
Be homey when you make the tea.

Talk of yourself and history,
embellishing with civility.
Of each story weave each thread
making your tapestry of the dead.

Frankenstein would run out on his bride
in order to find out where the monster hid.

The City of Angels impregnating March
with epic newness stands to liberty.
Thought and spoken books relieve the leaves
in evening's lattice of the loafing loved.
Read from an old page, an earlier age
studies even the warp in the blown glass
when history cracks, just like an earlier scene.
The mythic predecessors left their plans
in loach museums. Our newness runs with it.
We are no memory but vatic numbness,
Dracula's daughter is up and making tea,
in a textile print perhaps from Italy.
I am procrastinating, don't intend to write
anyone's last will and testament tonight.
The mood is intimate. Great aims at art
start with talk under statues where the stars
cast early sins in awkward flashing lights
or else with hauling finds back to small rooms
with music playing and zucchini cooking.
The artists come together in a troupe
and paint the poet's poems with their music.
Interacademically fine art
loves in the attics of the fairly rich
who have at least a hot dog,
in the troves of untouched treasure
that the eyes convey to fingers
in the halls where fine-eyed ladies take their coats.

Not the carpet, the floor.
At linespread, under talk
of Oedespeu, weird spew
word of Atlantic convo-
lutions meant to disfigure
the history lesson that had
come to pass. On the dawn
the effacive what is it
of his plans turned into
our older windowshade
of welcome, society
of word in print, his plan.
Semi-retiring the flashing
colors of his hurdles bit
into and slowly ate away
our resolve. He had brought
messages from other cities
to turn us under into our
own cessation, but for us.

When the wind has had enough it bangs
against the shutters, knocks the windowsill
of all your prowess lately where it hangs
in the low atmosphere for good or ill.
And all your words, your poems burst in the rain
wanting return, to open up the door
thence which they flew through first excluding pain
and now which stand and borrow from no more.
Your lines live in my eyes, in my handshake
that holds dissolving shadows of your time
as perfect prospects, foretold for the sake
of larger larks all turning on a whim.
The rain is roaring, but it is a fake
and all your hopes go turning on a dime.

My winter's sadness is no ice to break
upon steel trellises, slabs of concrete,
but inwards breaks upon me for my sake
enlifting and encumbering defeat.
I listen for the lighting of the lamps
and enter promptly on the outer ramps
with its view within. I am no one to go
to where the convalescent's cure is slow
but drop instead into the fallow fleet
reductive hollow where memories repeat.
The simple table rests upon and stamps
the cautious carpet where I hope to take
my will and testament out to the tramps
who sit and fish through ice-holes on the lake.

The Phantom of the Opera is fighting again
with the Hunchback of Notre Dame
about who is going to take out walking
Esmerelda in the rain.
Dr. Jeckyll and Mr. Hyde
are split on the issue of pride.
Dr. Jeckyll says "heck all"
where Hide would have just about died.
The invisible man doesn't want to be seen
unlike some tapdancing American.
The movies shine love as large as the moon
over the little desires of town.
All the unnoticed, the unexplored
porches and windows glow with fire
in the long dying afternoon
that glimmers thinly in the evening.
Someone could surely understand what I need,
as simple as the turning of a key,
recollection of the first drop,
and the opening of a door.

The ways of knowledge curl in a lattice
formation upwards. Every seat
below the moon is cursed with flowers
opening wounds in the late evening.
Spirit is colored and like wind it drifts
into the cottled streets. The shadows die,
the darkness unnoticed where they die.

My love breathes through its walls to you.
I can't replace the rocks and earth because
they for me now truly are you.

Unwelcome then mistakes, I sit alone
and count the umbrage of the wind my friend.
It's not so much that then I feel a slowing
as that I admire their end. I am complete
and would not stay another hour longer
but that the songs are good and the red wine
has opened up some windows in the shadows.

Unsmitten by the wind the toppling tasks
of other countries surface on the road
dividing traffic with their whims.
I have just returned from all my wins
and busted up inside need rest for bones.
There is a place to stop where surface seems
friendly as directions curtly grieve
to have you in the house where now we rest.

The rains make trouble for the older rains,
beating their tones into sanguinity.
The signal fades secluded in the mountains
where I've retuned to my virginity.
Suddenly realizing that my growing fame
glad I was impossible to define,
relieved me as I made love to my friend.
The older books—Yeats, Frost—still mostly care
and touch me in the place where I am one

with all of dream and love these twenty years.
The narrow gables inside still define
the people who have slept inside these rooms
or on the window seat have sat and wept.

When all red stain moneys sleep on trains
reversed in image where the raindrops bleat
while you are somewhere far off from the route I took
I think of you too staring at the rains
and wish that I were there to take the weight
of all your living, all I cannot say
each time you ask me how it is I love you
and I find I cannot say what way.

When all red satin monkeys sleep on trains,
alarm clocks broken, Porter disappeared,
I think you pulled a fast one on me Jane
and you should have at least let me explain
it was because I loved you I was there.
But you were quick and threw me on the train
before I had ideas of our daughter.
The rain collects stamps and has its own form of laughter,
rarely departing to give beneath the trees
its idea of splendour. Awaking a new man
I wanted to hear you sing and dance for me.

The Solway was their own particular hell,
each time the station loomed over the train
they reinitiated marriage vows
and went directly to the little steeple
where they had first made love, where you could see
his people's land. His friend's new death
had made the little mountain side curves steeper
and all the low tomatoes in the dark
feared for the coming time, the giant's step.
His son drew maps on blank white sheets of paper
that showed the drills and where the aircraft landed.
Chopin ruffled evening and the wine
drew scarlet patterns on the guests who dined.
I wish I had a photo of that day
to capture the brink of that society.
All we can now do is relive
the secret satisfactions of their love.

My poem is a huge poem shooting through my head
because my friend, a poet, shot himself dead.

Heaven haunting never enders
are cool pineapple ballet blenders
out of nowhere, once in a film saw go
into a grove of blind pretenders,
hand be their rooftops in the rain
under scrupulous shadows of stepping trees
where I pictured you under the magnolia.

Spring splinters plans with arduous showers of rain
through the electric shooting gallery
of god's own pinball send the lovers running
toward an imitation painted porch
where subdivision makes of darkness love.

Heaven wanted pineapple harbours
chocolate rains mango deep hours
for strawberry kisses to emerge from lime
where the old narcissus speeds no time
an instant pooling all our love and there
you are waiting in the outer where.

A tugboat postcards rock prismed sun
where no photography's begun.
The flags they wave are cherries of
the instant mind, no replica
but daft, aloft, sinking into
its own mind, its maple tree
of receptions, recognitions.

Each line I write unwrites its underwriting,
going backwards. Coming from the floor
am I. Welcome, undergraduates.
B-19. For me, return to dream.
Look at you. For you, a sheer hell.
My lady left me. Let's look before that
to when her peachy sheep dozed on the grange.
It glowed. You know it did. The town saloon.
Perhaps that day he hadn't cleaned his shirt
for trouble at the border stole some minutes
earlier in day's cooler avocado.
Now it was like a reception but also an announcement
which was perpetrated on his territory but also the other's,
so each one was standing sort of interfooted
on a mixed up vision of each other's land.
The rest was sheer excitement when his wife
took them all in and served them tonic crackers
and the town was told a thousand towns.
The wood creaked with some extra stolen hours
and the clocked ticked like hell all night long.

Frequently seldom sojourns at my aunt's
produced a strange desire to revert
to what I'd had been if I lived with them.
In the attic I found all the forgotten books,
chiefly Pogo, Mark Twain, and Agatha Christie.
I bird-watched with my cousin Fred
and slept above him in a bunk bed.

To do the big decision,
to exhibit in the exhibition,
provides in irrational apprehension
society's vulnerabilities.
The point of view is scattered, fragmented
in each appearance of his proposition,
best he could do at that late date recall
the schism that had made the total deeper.
From his tree house hill he watched the city,
and swept a cobweb off a daunted pepper.
By his own terms could say that he did well.

At sat around to implore your door
I snuffed my cigarette and then
your moonbeam animated face
lured me to heed its flickering signals
with their messages come deep from within,
the way a mailman delivers milk while you are sleeping.
The trees were sending vernal messages
about the buoyancy of night
the wind was rushing on your dress
your face had become red with cold.
I warmed you then and by the tree
your wet lips succumbed to me.

The Garlands of spring all on a string
drew sustenance of vernal 'tiquity
in the eye of purple chilled by night
where a dark jewess drew into the light.
The songs she sang were silvery and sad
and seemed to reach a higher heaven place
as pure as darkness when first love is real.
Strange shadows glowed and flickered on the ceiling,
dispersing scents of love letters from drawers
all tied in ribbons. The familiar clock
struck into night its stationary dock.
The lovers drift, wooing and stealing looks
and saying nothing, wanting to be alone.
At last they are alone, no need to speak
except in murmus, moans, or in low tones.
Light as the weather they touch.

The hook of dawn across the virgin city
revives a night's fantastic promises,
to see it real—the workers lifting steel,
the docks receiving ships, tall posters
arcing over the new light with phrases
said by chrysalis of light in winter
by the orphan without breath.
The dispersals of books, of rags of paper,
through the dark low streets might met with love
inspire a city of angels. Our new year.

Absolute fragment of his cooler suit
responded yearly to the sweet dismay
of his contemporary colleagues at the root
of the embellished weaving of his day.
He drives, but never he or we arrives.
I think that his subscription at the pool
is for the summer, when he lays around
addumbrating his history of the jews.
Often in or out, to smoke a pack,
there isn't very much that he would choose
to settle on, except Italian art,
or etudes of Chopin in half darkness.
The girl that loves him has enormous breasts
and slender hips, her blonde or brunette hair
has something in its nature of a dare
at bowling alleys or just in the car,
around the house she is meticulous
and seldom stops to read any of his mail.
She's far too busy looking so damn good
and entertaining guests who've been stopping by.

When all red satin monkeys sleep on trains
in over head compartments, and too
your porcelain rabbits sleep in shadowed glass
I think of many miles behind me you
by a window in rain, perhaps preparing food
or reading or singing in silvery mournful notes
and the queen of all bird song, all elegant courtesy.
I've seen you three times and every time felt that you
had something I need, something that made me glow
and tingle and smile and look at you
looking at me as though you understood
and felt the same way yourself.

In my pocket
bits of ice cream and lasagna
bits of crab meat and spumoni
in my wallet bits of bacon
slices of avocado wrapped in paper
against the sunrise and the tidal ocean.

It was different before
when the Christmas lanterns
shone your strange chances
in the mind of a distant manger.
*Three kings there were who travelled far
with gifts of gold for the new born.*

Innocently the ocean
hoists the harbour town into the rain storm
where in a rush hot coffee tastes better.
All we had to do was eat it up.
The rain storm on the outside
carries the ghost of Christmas tide,
and all is well in Bethlehem.

Can't have me any more at any price.
I just got tired. You're not loving me
was silly, was ridiculous, clown stuff.
They made your stories boring by default.
Yet still I love the dangling breasts of you,
the timid, crossed eyes, and the swagging saunter.
I just can't take this thing you have for christ
which comes between my teaching and loving you.
For after all although you're like a daughter
I am in love with a woman who's a mom.

Death Breath

Two shots of whisky vile
at midnight floating atop two Magner's.
I drank some water and later puked it up,
puked up twice the vile taste of whisky
which poisoning my tongue made my eyes cry.
Then the next night I order wrong, a guiness.
All dark thick creamy richness, heaviness.
I sank into a stupor with red eyes
held my stomach straight and only hicoughed.
I never brushed my teeth, and smoked a lot.

Shards of midnight cooing on the heath
are not more clever or more silver sad
than darkness glowing which envelops you.
Your hair mixed with magnolias stultifies
the progress of the time, its grandiose
insistence on the beats that measure out
the floating minutes of your searching thought,
these scents that are inducing memory,
the mantel clockpiece's stiff antiquity.
And now I am approaching the dark
because of all the women I have seen
you are the closest to my own ideal
and look like mine, my woman from the past,
nullifying the unnecessary.

The lights are doused upon the river towers
and I am left to unexplaining hours

The lights are doused and all the rabbits sleep
on different schedules. All around the house
the ghosts of might have been theres hound the roofs
and sputter in the gutters in the wind. The living room
blinds are drawn, and no one is within. Don't ring the gong.

I published lights, to haunt them with the shades
of previous incarnations, witnesses
to nothings of unrecorded history.
I brought the stillness of their suicides
crashing into realities of theirs
that lit up the place where you and I still walk.

The peanuts and the pretsels stank,
There wasn 't much with which I could fill up my tank,
I think that then my morale sank
because the pretzels rally stank.

The senses are deranged to begin with. The last call
of voices ripples the oyster horizon, feeds
the foretelling of your fall. In perfect silence
memory attenuates the senses
till all is still and real, examining
the buckle calendars, the rounded edges
of former prophecies, an island peace.
This projects an amber incandescence
into the center of the ductile leaning
that the heart misses, anatomical
invented ritual mimicking truth.

He solved the circle, and folded the sphere
into his thinking, flattened out the square
until his being mirrored what his seeing
had made of her.

My love like beaming light rides out across
lights of the city, far too late to go
home to the first woman that I knew,
still waiting for me in the earlier years.

The academy awards of my boners
line up to take their place
where I never wanted to address
someone who could hold me
what never really happened
and who I could caress
just as if it happened
holding out the stars
in a cool alignment
for you to drink success
from here till you undress
as if it had reminded
the clock upon the mantle
to let you go unreprimanded.

When all red satin monkeys sleep on trains
and porcelain donkeys of the slow parade
weap tears like cows of clouds is our romance
slated to renew this time of year
you sitting in your room, hoping I will call
me getting this dispatch off neanderthal
and I have done with all my nothing things
could come and stay with you when it turns spring
oh well, that will make it four years in a row
or have I counted an extra year as well.
Didn't know the history of your folks
but thought from your eye that it would be all right
if any of our secrets were told in the dark
or under one blanket in the darkening light.

When all red satin monkeys sleep on trains
and time turns sloward to the left behind
not even sleeping mirrored on the shelves
of rain that shed the town, shall we their sleeves
bear upward fellows fruit in argument
with the love goddess, with her elusive shake,
to deftly esymplate the thunder and take
of all her forward bloward toward floored.
Let fall the year. She is esemplatycally my dear
and will delay no dearer dear no more,
else what is she doing on the floor?
Her consequences of no proper deed
are beached on the moon ceiling where they can
elucidate the evening, like a fan
she shakes when she is looking at the dead.

After the bell rings, nothing rings the bell.
The town arrives, voices through the window
which carry words, His word, from far away.
The rustle of the wind in icy pines
soothes the cold ear that waited for the news
at home, where the shadows line the books
and voices fall from the not far off brooks.
A Word, His Word, you take like a sign
that crosses at the entrance where we've come.
Beyond is no need of books, where all books lie.
The tinsel voice will ring out in the window
and all He had to say then he will say.
We will return to darkness and in silence
I'll ask you about places far away
and you'll respond that that's where you first met me.

His interludes with girls had all gone wrong.
First Liz, the ingenue: "Don't look at me!"
who threw herself down across his bed
or asked to take a shower in his flat.
Then Cristine, the queen of goth morbidity,
hallucinating stalkers in the end.
Lisa, who he had each year in spring,
never believing that he loved her.
Then wanting him to call inexplicably.
And Kristen, who might call, or might not come.
Then I met a married Jewish girl
who I had met on several trips before
who always made me feel old kinds of love,
real kinds of love, like waiting for a story or a song
at night, or simply giving me her gifts.
I was three when the little girl in Gloucester
gave me a silver buddha, first gift of love
in all my ancient years. Those shadow these.
The urgency of knowing that when kindled
the hottest love is like an urgent sister
who tells your own heart to you, makes you strong.

All is now melancholy
but a false kind of melancholy
a look of pure understanding
silence of scattering words
not London not Paris
only possibly New York
Benjamin Paloff Don Share
Philip is our Apollinaire

Now all eyes are on the eye of love
the inward eye high above
the city and heart of silence
bringing back all memory
of the senses and of events

The girl I love gives me a gift
gives me something which is hers
a tiny silver elephant
dull and shiny like the fog
how my eyes long for her eyes
how my heart longs for her heart

There is nothing compared to her
except for poetry and friends
my secrets I can bear to her
and in silence make amends

Her dark eyes are silent streets
whose ends are blowing in the wind
I travel on. All falls away.
The childhood room begins again.
City of Angels. Arrival.

Her dark receptive tones
cut deep into my bones.

Lisa's sapphire eyes blow up with jellied rage
and bluer when she says, "No! Impossible!"
to all my protests. Four months later
I call her again at one. She's up.
"How did you know I wanted you to call tonight?"
Then later:
"If we were living in the same house together, I think we'd be on different floors."
"If we were living in the same house together!?" Much laughter.

In the darkness silver profiles
shuttle radiance of the seasons
and the clocks being reset
unto magnificence.

The wind in the trestle shudders as it did
when I mourned Cristina.
There is no passing of time.
I must be a saint for a week,
then meet my true love.

Meet her, now a doctor
with my hair half missing,
a poet by way of explanation,
whose (other) best friend just killed himself,
and who just finished his dissertation,
and for awhile had been banned from campus,
hearing voices for a year between
during which he wrote his recent chapbooks,
and readings in New York which she had attended.
Ready for the healing powers of love,
and strong from the battle he came away from,
She lead him into the darkened closet.
She is in love with him, and he knows it.

These unfelt feelings bristle with intake

perambulating out of the yard
the inmates bristle and a stiffer wind
exasperates groundskeepers on the wane
when bells told eight, shaking the cold breeze
and even dried out thistles of the trees.

The social comedy has its allures
and traps for man and woman in the know.
It pits the elder of the theatre arts
against the cheap illusions of the show.

Getting to know, is never really getting,
getting to know you in another setting,
spend the rest of the season betting.
Getting to know you is nothing,
is never really getting going, is everything
flowering in unknowing, train on train
of say an early German upbringing
around the piano, but of that the night
in all the silent blanket of its knowing,
all in the revealing of a heart.
Enthusiastically agreed
to what she wanted, raspberry crepes,
ordered after her hot chocolate,
I wasn't using any brakes.
What can you say after that?
Barred from campus,
my best friend killed himself,
seven months of hearing voices.
Three bad romances.

Because my love is like a silver star
and darkens rooms with intimacy
I must tell her that I love her
before my heart bursts with feeling it.

This is the new year that we so admired,
and this is the fruit and bounty of our glory,
commenceth here the singing of our story,
that what we wanted we have so inspired,
though singularly luck would have us vow
that we believe in our own beauty now.

This is the paradise of art and love
that has no need of easing up its flowing,
it is so excellent the place we're going,
to be returning the forgotten glove,
or lingering a moment where we entered,
as long as we agree that we are centered.

These are the senses that our sense imparted,
this is the epitaph of what we know,
the voices now are flowing that must go,
this is a country that shall be uncharted,
forever forth to which we shall belong,
in our devotion to this simple song.

Frankenstein was idle on the lands
his fathers buried. Thelma takes his hands
and promises a child, a Frankenstein,
and wedding bells with bubbles of champagne.
But he is old and tired, and he is mired
in his work, digging in the graveyard.

Arnold comes but once a year,
full of Christmas joy and cheer,
drops his coat and sheds his scales,
well admiring the whales.

Little Arnold, Arnold gruff,
not your ordinary stuff,
all the girls cry out enough
when Arnold gets into the rough.

Underneath the poking tree
Arnold did to two or three
what you must only do to one,
making arrangements for a son.

Now Arnold has his choice of brides,
often exploring their insides,
and though he comes but once a year
Arnold is full of Christmas cheer.

Snaggly incarnated as a movie star,
film noir, and gala opening, jaguar car,
lost in jugular amplitudes of after hours,
glistening from the ceiling's stars,
elbows in calendar corners of paper headlines,
the explosive double on the mind, the trap
an adhesive armstrap, all kinds of other crap
too numerous to split along these lines.
When you answer me I move slightly forward
but pulled back also, until you ease me further.
She was seven when she lost her father,
but do go on, and come back to it later,
let's both be floored.

The academy awards of my boners
line up to take their place
where I never wanted to address
someone who could hold me
what never really happened
and who I could caress
just as if it happened
holding out the stars
in a cool alignment
for you to drink success
from here till you undress
as if it had reminded
the clock upon the mantle
to let you go unreprimanded.

Each time you slap at the sheets
I hear the sound of dirt on the floor
the blankets open like a whale
too late to keep my shinnies cold.
The sun is your morning of headlines
and I am picking dandelions
and nothing could be any finer
except returning on a steamer.
The late clocks tolled the memory home.
The nursing homes were without a visit.
The phantom of the opera came,
asking everyone what is it?
But from my vantage on the floor,
I couldn't really see him any more,
and so as I have been inclined to fidget
I'll add only that I roast your window
and that tonight the stars are following me.

Yes, seeing is wanting and talking
Yes, I take my gun out all of nights
charming color chimes the ceiling
exhorting years like nineteen nine
to spill their beans You were very pretty
I thought it especially appreciated
your low keyed smell and the dark cover
you afforded out of my mind you're nice
but someone really ought to tell your tailor
who you are dressing for besides his taste
can reach the moment of high tremolo
where you would meet upon this face to face
that clown your father falls across the stairs
and I am hidden in a whitewashed orchard
welcoming winds or rats have word of you
is it really you coming through the shadows

The rain is falling, but you're asleep
and will not see me sitting here
while all my mind fills up with snow
like breathing of stars in the dark.
There's little here that I don't know,
and there's no reason for me to leave,
the beauty shines as bright as God,
and I have all I'd ever need.

Sometimes on the island veering off
the road into the forest headlights crash
perform surgery on rare old trees
while those the living slow our traffic down
and hardly ever get anywhere on time
except for a drunken party with no end.
Still the beauty of the mangled lights
inspires a love like that for shuttered windows,
for bodies laid out in state but out of view,
who never got to know where they were going
or coming from, murdering squirrels in the dark.

Your puppetry, dear mother marionette,
is suitable displayed in ornament,
and the front lighting of the glassed in stage
magnificent for telling of an age.
The first time I saw you, my heart beat wildly and
your silver voice of an angel sang me to sleep.
The second year I saw you was much more deep
because you sat next to me in the bruncheon parlour
and leaning toward me invited me to the museum.
My fault! Idiot! I never called you back.
Now two years later you are so beautiful
letting me share an order of crepes with you,
and scolding me for not calling you back.
You found the rusty key that turns my heart,
something you gave me that belonged to you.
Now in the passion of short telephone calls
to arrange to see you, you: "I want to see you"
my friend calls me and tells me when to come.
All Russians, except my friend and me.
Well, he's a Russian, but speaks the King's English.
Nevertheless I'm drowned in Russian sounds
and follow my love's progress with my eyes,
She sits across the yard in the old shed,
and smokes and looks at me across the way
framed in the window, and she winks at me.
She's married, but well I am in love.
I must go to New York and see her again.

Emily with white gloves and long black hair,
and fairest skin, and piercing deep brown eyes,
became my girl when I was seventeen
and she was just sixteen, a junior then.
I waited for her in the lonely night
trying to find the words to get it right.
She was there, o how she was there
and came to me while the day was still light.
The other centuries then showed surprise,
when she showed me her photos in the parlour,
or when we turned out the lights in the den,
listening in the dark to Charlie Parker.
In Providence we stayed with her brother Adam,
and found old 78s of early jazz
we listened to all morning, Holy morning!
After a night of love-making in Providence,
to which I haven't returned in 26 years.
The night she was mine, I threw her in the snow
and crying shouted Emily Emily Emily I love you
until she gave in and let me kiss her.
From that moment on she was my girl,
and I was proud to take her everywhere,
to be invited to dinners at her house,
such a collection of books, music, and questions.
I was Rimbaud, and hardly said a word.
Emily, my sponsor, spoke for me.
She kept my poems and wouldn't give them back,
for months and months, so many written for her.

The skies are morning and I have no need to sleep
the car wheels grate along the rainy roads
like winches raising or lowering a bridge
the one I love is sleeping in her bed
in lovely restfulness knowing the day awaits

There is no trick or tack I wouldn't try
to find myself in her company again
it's like an addiction this need to cry
on the shoulder of my chosen woman
whose sad eyes are bright with kindness
with telling jokes that also make me laugh

Like Philip says you could stick pins in my ass
a Russian proverb for sure when my own love
is standing there laughing along with him
She just might like to do that and she might
allow a little nibble or a bite
but I am dreaming of immortal love
and want to take her with me high above

Though he arrived
his presence is not felt
inside the sleeping town
before ice melt
and the docks steam
with new activity
under the protection
of the sea

Only in memory
his thoughts revive
the promise when
his friend was still alive
and like a chrysalis
all forms abstain
from commentary
turning into rain

He is the one
whose name will echo through
provincial palaces
of well to do
consignatories
of a new regard
like kisses melting
into radiant art

Though he arrived his presence is not felt
inside the sleeping town before ice melt
and the docks steam with new activity
under the protection of the sea

Only in memory his thoughts revive
the promise when his friend was still alive
and like a chrysalis all forms abstain
from commentary turning into rain

He is the one whose name will echo through
provincial palaces of well to do
consignatories of a new regard
like kisses melting into radiant art

In the proud panning enormity
of the city laid out like a wreath
the present passes like an echo of
models that resurrect a century
while lights sweep by and houses scarcely breathe
under the ruins of our musical
endowment of hope and faith and history.

Tonya my senses blare into my hearing
a kind of language that I recognize
have been prepared for since my infancy

The star of night is shining in its boxes
The little bird is singing on its wing
The windows spiders shadows elephants

I scarcely know what words to use to tell
of how I feel, or what I think I know.
It's not that recently I've been through hell;
it doesn't even feel like that is so.

I scarcely know what words to use to tell
of how I feel, or what I think I know.
The old familiar streets all still foretell
the long unfolding vignettes that we go
to so much trouble for. Strange rooms enclose
the other lives we long to hear and see,
whether anyone watches, comes or goes.
I don't think that I would like to be
any of those. My close friend's suicide
is fine with me now. Four times in four years
I saw the girl I love and then I cried.
But this time she is filling me with ideas,
our hearts draw closer, and the gun is filled.
Now we decide together what is killed.

The Marriage Certificate

I need to know your middle name,
your date of birth, and your maiden name,
if you have a maiden name.
The elephantine gargoyles of jade on the wall
protrude vociferous assent on what they're bent on.
The jellied curries cool in marble shells.
Equations are donuts. Last time evening spooled
a night like this, the chef de maitre drooled
on Preston Sturges' lens. The shadows blather
their foreign ether. Intimate uncoil
the jealous jellies of a maiden's eyes.
Wallpaper eavesdrops. Shiny the wainscots
remember similarities. I am
a fool. I have been never happier.

I would celebrate by reviewing Katia's book.
I was about to celebrate,
but they want to postpone my defense.
I thought I was a doctor of Philosophy.
Sure enough I will be.
But for now, there's little but this
impossibility of getting away to New York
for the kinds of reasons you can imagine.
But there, put in a quiet room, with some
Italian opera playing low, *Santa Lucia*,
I would sit with someone who I know,
and be transported to the other world
of little soldiers marching in the snow.
Blessed and ordained. That would be nice.
Our own two person progress and project
and epiphantic harmony with night,
with love and our own parlour game.

Ice kindled tree to life in passive fog.
The shadows settled on the wires log
too absent early. Then he heard eavesdrop
the marching others hush and the wind stop.
Behind was only no one then he had
rented wrongly regulated flat.
Fat chance a father, earwig flowing
like a cape over him owing
nothing. When announced to him as Kris
regarded other nowhere near the roof
saying to him, this is how it is,
I hope this will be brotherly enough.
Chimney fallows. Blast black in the knit
changes. Rectangularly repeat.

March evaporates the granite rains
by stellar axis, fellowing the clouds
and making references to former pains
along the treetops and above abodes
where nothing happens, or a library
allows a glimpse of muslin corners where

March evaporates the granite rains
along the rooftops, where nothing detains
the idle moonlight peeking through the clouds,
and by the stellar axis of their shrouds
climbs down enormous branches of a tree
a muslin corner of the library
glimpses, where unfettered in the wind
the new year pricks the hearing of the blind,
and passes through demented promises
although it is not yet the time for kisses.
His is the first arrival into town
whose empty visit is being born.
The crystal fixity of vacuous
haste at what is it that it is
devolves no answer, yet it is a crown.
So he set out to make the town his own.

The tree bark bristles and the stiff air echoes
but there is not the promise of a ghost
present to witness nothing how it goes
now that there is formerly a past.
They sleep unwaiting. Shall the voices grow
to meet him on this question? Will he know
angelic reason as he claims to now?
He believes it because it is so.

Tonya the burning armour of my heart
boils in oblivion, roses shimmer so
when I wake dreaming

Another year goes by and you are gone

Another year goes by and you're not here

Your white budded breasts are ships at sea

So long as I have known you I have known

Tonya, don't look at me when I speak my verse,
but look inside whatever Russian plains
still hold your thought in this America,
or find the matter of the water to be little good
even across from where your apartment stood
off Broadway by Columbia. We met
four times and yet

Five times now have I met the girl I love.
What is the use of keeping to myself

Last night while you were rustling through the cans
I tried to warn you not to go through mine.
Writing this to you wasn't in my plans,
but since we're at it, to avoid a fine
for both of us, and to appease my mind,
will you in future please refrain from taking
the boxes marked in yellow. If I find
that there is any problem I'll be fucking
out to murder you. Having said that,
I don't mind if you drop by to say hi.
On Saturday someone gave me a hat
which is just your size. I mean it please stop by.
You may have messed things up with my landlord
but I have ways to make you really bored.

Surfing the net I saw a friend had died, had taken his life,
a few hours before. I saw him there, crumpled to the ground.
It all over. His brain spattered blood. His arms
lifeless because the great body that carried him
over the fields and the sand dollar lakes.
Sweet angel don't stop me till I sing my song.
Could it be true? I suspected murder. A plot
to get a hold of his rare manuscripts,
which fortunately he had burned, leaving copies with me.

Night rare night where clustering the stars
the moon

The functional intrinsic mechanism
of evening shudders and makes little room
for clustered carpets shaking out a broom
down through the caskets of yards, oblivion
which is our city, atavistic prayer
to the same brickloads and a painted wall
that shined upon this modern sortilege
three memories ago where all the same
the geographic patterns spelled a name
and tins of liquids spelt out on the shelf
a kind of prayer of hope and sacrifice.
These scatter in the wind like dried out husks
and plants cold seed in generations' dirt.
The winds are ceilings, ornamented clouds
spatter green light, spatter magenta light,
the city hold its promises silently.

What I mean not what I wish to say

I haven't masturbated since I met you.
Nor for a moment do I forget you.

The iron maiden of your breast
makes me pray to east and west.

For everyone else there is a word
not keptly felt, not feltly kept, knotted
"O its a printing press!" is what I heard
no great secret, no longer addressed
butter remember Emily
sad to be

Am I changed? Am I a new man?
Am I in debt now to a woman?

I don't care. Because I'm blooming
independent I am fuming.

Often nature takes its course.
Why then should I feel remorse?

I am paid a sailor's wage.
Spending money stifles rage.

Most of the time it's ship to shore,
making friends who I abhor.

Admit that in her company
I have been a degree more free.

Inescapably her scent
often asks me what I meant.

And her hair is like a tiara
that I purchased in Samsara.

When all red satin monkeys sleep on trains
in overhead compartments, mirroring
the passing landscape, somewhere in the rain
back in the city you prepare to sleep.
Your passing thought of me deflects the wind
and sinks into a swamp passing the land.
I'd be with you, and stay there if I can,
long as you'd have me in your neighborhood.

A frozen crystal spectrum magnified
and seen though eyelets of the older trees
along the sleepless streets down in the rain
that winds about a private library

there is no one

Love's disappointment or was it not love's
he couldn't venture, had no need to speak

The crystal needles raining on the town
expand the sky in pockets where the fog
slides downstreet, and the sky is full of eyes
not listening, where no one ever goes.
Sleep purchases the windows and the lights
that trail through fingers of the passing time
inside the library, where no one goes
except for boats of pounding rain that drag
across the roof and hammer on the roof.
There is no way a visitor subsides
in contemplation getting the full size
of other hands, of places that they go
to lift a moment suddenly in view
where every passenger is someone new.

This is Miss Insley. Show her to her room.
She takes her tea at four. She bathes at nine.
She'll spend her afternoon in the lyceum,
checking up on other people's work.
She never tells a lie. She dropped the phone
and didn't call back. Someone took her name.
I think it's madness. Rest awhile then try
the garage door. Excuse me, sir. I'm tired
of trying. What you want it for? Myself.
I didn't recognize the number, so
I did what is it, told them. How'd you know?
I didn't think so, but I think it's so.

Dull to dumb,
how come?
Never said,
went to bed.
But what is it
is exquisite
beyond compare
there, where.

Between the minutes echo as they beat
the streetlight, words I heard him say so
yellow magnolia, traffic red and green

Not knowing you isn't a criterion for stopping
the flow of you into the semiandroidable
rocking future: your exact song and smile
adobe crescents wind too high to chime
semianderable hush aloft the scullions

Beneath the slopes of silver hang the lines
that rise over the horizon down below
where architectural lozenges expand

When I walked out to town
why did you think I see?
Cassandra Nelson's frown
all over the A.B.C.
I didn't think that that
could stop the London flow
from Russell Square down to
Victoria. The old man who?
He built a steam engine
with a sterno flame
and sent her clippings
of his politics, all local,
built on the historic city.

Sort of skyrockets of placid calm
tap the inertia of eternity
in liquid minutes blown over the dawn
and people waiting. The sloping estate
winds through their woulds,
and leaves only an impression,
but against its angular recalcitrance

You and she and we
are writing poetry.

Thank you very much, and all the same
I've no desire now for company
but hers.

How I wish I could go back
to Emily at seventeen.

Do I Know You?

To love you I have to know you,
but what I know you will never know,
and what I know is what I know of you,
to know the world, to love to know
to know to love, and by loving me
love to be loved, the only way of knowing.

The wind approaches, the wind and the rain
the town is castled on a peak of stone
Silent sublunary lexicons of jade
break up the seconds, in a swirl of notes
not heard but seen like architecture
breaking perspectives, attaching to

the patterned marble floor, the ante paid,
a swirl of references, of tumbling notes
each meaning the silence, the silence meaning
what he thought, a miracle of jade
passed through the moments, fractured in the rain
that beats against the attic, writes on the roof

tumbling attention, volleys of preannouncing jade
disturbing the storm clouds, on a ledge's way
announcing visit, and the visit paid
in ethereal room of pallets, card tables
where all of the pennies are the same
broken in minutes, like the sound of rain.

Silence if a lexicon of jade
returning the minutes, silent revival
of memories of sound spilt in the vacant
hesitancy of a game of cards
where it is played to while away the hours
waiting for the wind and the rain.

The hour of decision before bed
sliding toward sleep, oblivion of time
The wind and rain approach a peak of stone
symphonically the years go falling down
and turn about a single window lit
the library where a young couple makes love

The crosses forbid visitors, and world of books
and paintings stimulates the sense
of passing time, of the substance of art,
when very quickly snow is snowing down
where time is watching with its older views
and breaking up the card game now for sleep

In Mrs. Gardener's boudoir
we smoked hashish and drank champagne
on Christmas eve. Below, the choir
of off-guard duties rendered pain
among the Singers, while we played
a Chopin prelude, improvised,
manic, on Paderewski's frayed
piano, which was ill-advised.

I am the one whose journey through the woods
takes him across borders, past windowsills
where the unsuspecting townspeople sleeping
have left their trays on sills, their candles sleeping,
thought only by the wind as it is passing.
I come at nighttime when the windows shine
within with noisy solaces, with signs
of life such as you will meet in the day,
on your first morning, your arrival dawning.
Christ shines prismatically in shards of ice
that goes unnoticed otherwise, in view
to the strange traveller who on rain steps
past libraries of the wolves and hounds,
buried in darkness, family or spring.

I have returned from far across the land
where a chrysalis in mediation
I saw my future spread before me like a plan
in a slow time of poverty and suffering.

The streets were filled with ghosts of Matt and Kate,
no longer in the city. It was late;
I sliced my finger on the garden gate,
and slowly entered, rising to the bait.
Something in your eyes replacing thought
fixed my confusion. The chocolate I brought
lay on the kitchen table. I made you wait
alone in the bed. Everything I sought
was there, and when you fixed me with your eyes
I understood that everything dies.
There were words I could no longer say,
thinking to leave them for another day,
and only now to hold you in my arms,
receptive only to your ageing charms
that overwhelmed me. Having what you want
is so surprising that it tends to daunt
the will, dividing every loving face.
Emotionally I couldn't leave the place,
but stay, even now. Nothing can replace
the weight of your refusals, suddenly
denied and lifted so that I could see
the unspeakable sadness of your love for me.

How many years, and yet with no routine,
these are things that sometimes I have seen.

Alone with my love, there isn't much to say.

April to May again. In bed with you,
after a year now, third year in a row,
is more now, more defined what is it,
something irreplaceable. You there,
choosing now for me to make my visit.
Myself, in love with you as never before.

The Posthumous Sonata rips and shakes
my memory; was I here before?
I feel your foot, no longer on the floor,
and go on talking. I knew that you loved
me, but wonder if you know (of course you do).
It isn't that you're pretty, though you are
(extremely, who could paint that shade of blue?),
more that you're beautiful, the way you tilt
the word you are at me, the way I heard
the pure intention of unspoken love.
We have our springs, a deep, familiar thing.
Not what you answer (still we listen to).
Yes yes. I will mirror you until
you let me love you, till you do too.

There was no other way of speaking to her,
no matter what they say or how they view her.
What is love, beauty? Does she know, or does he?
Attraction and familiarity
go a really long part of the way,
but does she see
how alive is he?

Love affairs have all turned bad,
nicest girl I ever had
only loves me once a year.
Rest of the time I am here.

Her name is Lisa, now you know
the vocables I beckon to.
Someone tell her she loves me
(even though it is plain to see).

Every spring is every spring
I can remember, every blooming spring.
Then I can get her to sing.
The rest of the year is drear.

Lisa, see me in the winter time.
When we have warmed each other in the cold
you'll know I am the husband for you,
in the darkness, in the cold.

After a year of my trips to New York, Matt and Katy were leaving New York,
and Lisa for the third April in a row led me through the hand
getting off in Williamsburg, Brooklyn. Her apartment was tiny,
on the first floor and filled with cats looking out of the screens.
I thought of how all had been good for me, how New York'd changed,
how Lisa was my prize possession, the pleasure I lived for,
the triumph, denoument,

She is as is as any is as is.
She wis an wis as any wis an wis.
Shock do she is. Supracease
is winesglow. Certecease
is hindsglow. Supracease
is nisit. Nisir et nisit.
Supracease et nisit.
Windsglow. Hindsisit.
She is an wis, as any wis an wis.

Strange how love flows over the half-lit skies
like so much time lost, settling in your eyes.

The Author

Ben Mazer was born in New York City in 1964. His poems have been widely published in international periodicals, including *Fulcrum, Verse, Harvard Review, Jacket, Agenda, Stand, Boston Review, Salt,* and *The Wolf*. His poetry collections include *Poems* (Pen & Anvil Press, 2010), *White Cities* (Barbara Matteau Editions, 1995), and two chapbooks, *The Foundations of Poetry Mathematics* (Cannibal Books, 2008) and *Johanna Poems* (Cy Gist Press, 2007). He is the editor of *Selected Poems of Frederick Goddard Tuckerman* (Harvard University Press, 2010), Landis Everson's *Everything Preserved: Poems 1955-2005* (Graywolf Press, 2006, winner of the first Emily Dickinson Award from the Poetry Foundation), and a forthcoming edition of the poems and critical prose of John Crowe Ransom. He lives in Boston, where he is a contributing editor to *Fulcrum: An Annual of Poetry and Aesthetics.*